Jewelry
by
CHANEL

PATRICK MAURIÈS

Jewelry
by
CHANEL

Thames & Hudson

Jean Cocteau: drawing from
an unpublished portfolio,
c. 1933.

Translated from the French by Barbara Mellor
Picture research by Marianne Francuzik

First published in the United Kingdom in 1993 by Thames & Hudson Ltd, 181A High Holborn, London WC1V 7QX

© 1993 and 2000 Thames & Hudson Ltd, London. Text © 1993 Patrick Mauriès. First paperback edition 2000

British Library Cataloguing-in-Publication Data, a catalogue record for this book is available from the British Library

ISBN 0-500-28055-X

Printed in Hong Kong by H&Y Printing Limited

Contents

Introduction

It was Roland Barthes who, never averse to a neologism, invented the happy concept of '*bathmologie*', or the science of degrees. And the finest possible example of this science, as applied to the art of jewelry, is to be found in the work of Chanel. The impulse to 'take a step backwards from a remark, a sight or a body so as to turn any response to it that we might have had completely on its head', to shift our priorities, deny the obvious and confound our expectations: this is the motivating force that urges on all 'bathmologists', whether they be rigorous intellectuals or dedicated socialites, required inexorably to be different. It was the definition of fashion itself, as we know, which provided Chanel with her 'first degree', the initial step or bottom rung in her career: the conventional reading of fashion as a sign of distinction, a status symbol, a good investment, a symbol of affluence, a statement of wealth and a declaration of social acceptance; as a sort of visible shorthand, in essence, of the wearer's position on the social ladder. This was the difference in which lay Chanel's popular appeal: shifting everything up a notch, she systematically turned on their heads all the accepted principles of conventional elegance, replacing over-rich textures with more ordinary materials, decorative intricacies with a simple line, and an overabundance of significant detail with a total absence of it. This was to be her strategy, which she was to follow even more resolutely in her costume jewelry – where she made a virtue of making counterfeits out of the genuine article, and endowing the counterfeit with its own worth – than in her clothes.

Christian Bérard: Chanel
her model, Indian ink drawing,
c. 1930.

This aversion to snobbery, this indifference in the face of 'the false flattery of the looking glass' as Proust described it, formed the constant foundations of Chanel's style throughout her career: a designer of jewelry full of paradoxes, she was obsessed with a desire for genuineness and an inability to accept anything smacking of imitation. This was to be the eternal counterpoint to her notion of 'style', of whatever could be taken to represent the average, the shared experience or common denominator of an age. There is not room enough here to list all the quotations, the remarks and the throw-away lines that Chanel took a provocative delight in casually tossing out, fostering that same dry wit, that same whittled-down style that became her trademark: elegance was 'a sacrifice, a rooting out of excess. A slip, a button, a millimetre of cuff or a flounce. It is a whole philosophy. . . . It means good clothes which look good'; 'luxury is what cannot be seen';[1] 'this frantic desire to dazzle people sickens me'.[2] She was always obsessed with avoiding ostentation, or anything that seemed to be setting out to make a statement or create an impression. To lay stress on this principle in the introduction to a glittering collection of precious stones – the first study of Chanel's taste in the sphere of jewelry, in which (making use in turn of another inversion) we intend to discuss 'real' jewels where 'fake' ones might have been expected – may thus seem paradoxical. And indeed it would be so, if this discussion were to be limited only to the first impression of the very definition of elegance according to Chanel. For this definition does not rest simply on an inversion

Christian Bérard: Chanel
baring her exhibition of jewelry,
Indian ink drawing, 1932.

2

of opposite poles, a substitution of the counterfeit for the genuine article, or an affectation of tokens of poverty or meagreness, but it depends rather, as will become clear, on a confusion of the definitions of these two poles, on a shifting of the basic premise of the notion of elegance, and on a restoration of all its original power and lustre to the idea of luxury.

The tastes of Chanel offer a precise reflection of her life. Rarely has the story of a life – in this case recounted so often – been so closely interwoven with the transformation of a sensibility and the evolution of a style. Disposed as she always was to come away with something from every encounter, Chanel seems to have retained a nuance or an inflexion from each of her relationships, later blending them into a specific style. Her life was made up of layers laid one on top of the other, cut through by presences and passions of an exceptional nature; none of her friends or lovers was ordinary, and all have left their mark. And there is something strangely intriguing in the thought that our tastes, our notions of elegance, should still, over half a century later, be influenced by a few love affairs embarked upon by chance in the 1920s and 30s by a handful of men who left as strong a mark on Chanel as she did on them.

Lovers on the one hand (Balsan, Boy Capel, Westminster, Dimitri and others), friends on the other (Cocteau, Stravinsky, Picasso and others): the story of the evolution of Chanel's aesthetic bears this double stamp, and it was her jewelry which, perhaps more manifestly than her fashion designs, was to pay tribute to this network of influences.

In the mythology of her life that Chanel has left to posterity, she accords first place quite unambiguously, not to Etienne Balsan, the gentleman farmer of solidly French roots, sturdy values and equestrian tastes who nevertheless came first in strictly chronological order, but rather to the Englishman Boy Capel, whose early death in December 1919 was to leave a void in the young designer's life which the passing years never succeeded in filling. Boy it was, clearly, who initiated Chanel in the ways of the fashionable world, bringing about an admirable improvement in the matter of elegance, and giving rise to the celebrated remark which has been quoted ever since: ' "Since you are so attached to those clothes that you always wear," Capel used to say to me, "I shall have them remade more elegantly by an English tailor." That was the beginning of everything that ever came out of the Rue Cambon.'

This note of Englishness, a sense of elegance that was as manifest as it was invisible, a morbid dread of being overdressed, a loathing of well-regulated, self-satisfied chic – these were the principles embodied by Capel, and which inspired Chanel's *modus operandi*: 'I cut an old jersey down the front so as not to have to pull it on over my

Christian Bérard: portrait
of Coco Chanel,
Indian ink drawing,
c. 1930.

dress. I sewed a ribbon on here . . . I added a collar and bow there. Everyone went wild

over it. . . . They asked me how much it was. I said I would have to find out. I sold ten of

those dresses instantly. My dear, my fortune was founded on that old jersey that I put

on because it was so cold in Deauville. . . .'[3]

These were the principles of an aesthetic created from the fact that 'two men

were fighting over my small person'. A third, ten years older, then arrived to confirm

this taste for elegance, or rather for detachment. It was to her affair with the Duke of

Westminster, in about 1925, that Chanel attributed her love of tweeds, and she traced

the inspiration for her matelot top and beret – a severe look which became

inseparable from the first appearances of those strings of pearls which were to

become an essential part of her trademark – to a number of trips on his yacht, the

Cutty Sark.[4] 'If I hadn't met Westminster', she used to say, 'I would have gone out of

my mind. I was too agitated, there was too much going on. . . . I left for England

in a daze. With Westminster there was nothing to be done. My life began because I

calmed down.'[5]

During her seven years (which she calmly extended to thirteen) with the richest

man in England, she was introduced to a life of the most unbridled luxury, a style of

life that was veritably royal ('I have known luxury on a scale that no one will ever

experience again'). It was this which doubtless led her to believe that she had

experienced every possible variation of *savoir-vivre*, every shade and nuance of elegance, before finally transcending the interplay of the different social classes with their different values, all of them relative, in order to arrive at a formula that was absolute, a subtle mixture of simplicity and extravagant excess. Still in the 1920s, it was with the Grand Duke Dimitri, the fourth note in this sentimental chorus, that she honed to perfection her sense of opulence. Grandson of Tsar Alexander II, nephew of Alexander III, first cousin of Nicholas II, all he had ever known, despite a lonely childhood, was the splendour of a profligate court, which fascinated Chanel to the point of influencing her collections at the time. He offered a dazzling counterpoint to the languidness of English elegance and the restrained charm of French taste, while also giving her the opportunity to indulge a fondness for the less happy taste of a prince of the blood. . . .

With the exception of Boy Capel, to whom she was never bound by any exchange of gifts, each of these amorous episodes was punctuated by some gem of symbolic significance, which together spun a glittering thread through Chanel's life. When she and Balsan parted she returned all his gifts, keeping only a gold ring set with a topaz – a stone for which she always professed a special fondness – which stayed with her to the end of her life. Dimitri for his part presented her with a gold necklace which she can be seen wearing in the most celebrated photographs of her from the 1930s. And finally, and most famously, it was during a cruise that the Duke of Westminster, seeking her forgiveness for some real or imagined transgression, gave her an emerald,

which she dropped overboard, like 'Cleopatra dissolving Caesar's pearls in vinegar'[6].
These stones, whether milestones or mementoes, lost or given, sound like so many
notes in a prelude: Chanel opened her hat business in Deauville in 1912, but she did
not start showing jewelry until twenty years had passed: twenty years of adventures
and affairs, at the close of which there rose the imposing figure of Paul Iribe. With
Etienne de Beaumont, François Hugo and Fulco di Verdura, Iribe was to be one of the
principal protagonists in the story of Chanel's jewelry.

Part One

The importance of the part that Iribe was to play in Chanel's life and his determining influence on the conception and execution of the jewelry that she launched in the 1930s are justification enough for lingering a while over the otherwise familiar course of Iribe's career, and a life of which hardly a moment seems to have been without its significance.

The story of Iribe's life is above all the story of a passion for France. His father, Jules Iribe, had returned to Paris – having been forced to go into exile because he had taken part in the dismemberment of the Vendôme column during the Commune – only three years before Paul's birth, on 8 June 1883. Having spent part of his adolescence in Madagascar, where his father had acquired a lease on some land, the young Paul returned to Paris to continue his studies.

Despite a lack of enthusiasm on his part, he was apprenticed as a typographer on the daily newspaper *Le Temps*, of which his father had been made editor. This period was clearly decisive for the development of his tastes, since a significant part of his activities throughout his life was to be inspired by a passion for printed matter in all its forms, from newspapers to de luxe editions. He very soon demonstrated an interest in graphics, and his first satirical drawing appeared in *Le Rire* on 23 March 1901. In the decade that followed he was to do work for all the leading illustrated journals of the day, from the *Assiette au Beurre* to *Le Canard Sauvage*, by way of *Le Rire*, the *Illustré National* and so forth. In 1906 he started his first periodical, *Le Témoin*, in which he

Jean Cocteau:
Poiret departs, Chanel arrive
drawing, 1926/28.

14

Jean
✦

'Labs'
Poiret s'éloigne –
Chanel arrive

gave expression to an often savagely satirical view of his age, along the lines of the German *Simplicissimus*.

With its exceptional graphic style (he was able to employ the best illustrators of the time) and its searing social and political criticism, *Le Témoin* sealed Iribe's reputation. But his interests could not be confined to satire in its various forms, or to a painful awareness of the state of the nation; he had always been fascinated by the apparent antithesis to himself, to the realms of luxury and elegance, sophistication and frivolity. Having had his attention caught by the early issues of *Le Témoin*, in 1908 Paul Poiret went to see Iribe: 'I told Iribe about a plan I had to produce a beautiful book, aimed at the highest levels of society, which would be a collection of drawings by him of my dresses, to be printed on the finest Arches or Dutch paper and intended as a sort of homage to all the *grandes dames* of the world. Then I showed him some of my dresses in order to see his reaction. He went into raptures. "I have often dreamed of dresses such as these," he told me, "but I could never have imagined that someone had already created them. They are su-perb, and I want to set to work im-med-iate-ly; I also want to introduce you to an as-ton-ish-ing woman, infinitely distinguished, who will wear these quite di-vine-ly." '[7] Thus it was that the celebrated album of *Robes de Paul Poiret* saw the light of day, the first of a series of de luxe editions which were to spangle Iribe's career (*Nijinski* in 1908, *L'Eventail et la fourrure*, published by Paquin in 1911, and in the 1930s *Rose et Noir, Blanc et Rouge, Choix, La Marque*

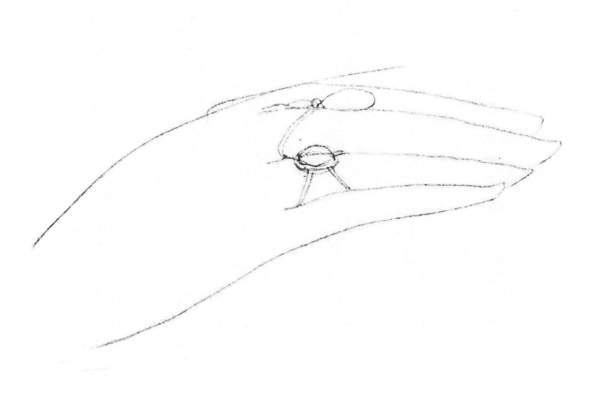

Iribe: page from a sketchbook,
study for a ring,
1925/30.

France, *Défense du luxe* and *Sourire de Reims* among others, all published by Draeger).

In 1910, the same year in which *Le Témoin* ceased to appear, Iribe branched out in a new direction, and one with a direct connection with the chapter of his life that is of most interest here. He drew up some jewelry designs for the goldsmith Robert Linzeler, which the latter carried out, exhibiting the finished pieces in December 1911. In an article written for *Vogue* fourteen years later, Linzeler identified the lines of force of this new approach (also discussed in an article by Robert Carsix in *Art et Décoration* of January 1911, quoted in Bachollet *et al.*, p. 103), anticipating some of the characteristics which were to become cornerstones of Chanel's jewelry designs in the 1930s: 'He exerted his influence in two different areas. Firstly in the matter of size. In all his drawings showing women's hands the rings were always set with large stones. Then in his decorative approach. When he began to put together arrangements that were really going to be carried out, when he had these most dazzling and sumptuous of materials before him, he immediately saw the possibilities they offered. . . . And yet very few of these designs have been carried out, so that the public at large is not familiar with their novelty and their variety.'[8] An exceptional sense of proportion, a taste for unrestrained splendour, the juxtaposition of stones and textures, a new definition of settings: these were just some of the remarkable features which were to be found two decades later in the jewelry of Chanel.

Following this excursion into the realm of precious stones, Iribe turned his hand to designing interiors (for Jacques Doucet in 1912), stage productions and textiles (including a silk design for Bianchini Férier), as well as to what was to be his chosen field, advertising. After the First World War – during which, in company with Cocteau and Misia Sert, he had helped to organize aid to the wounded – he went to New York. There he opened an interior design shop, before going to work from 1920 to 1925 for Hollywood and Cecil B. de Mille, for whom he supervised eight films.

On his return to France in 1927 he took up his interior design and advertising work again, launching the series of special and de luxe editions published by Draeger which have already been mentioned. His private life was marked by his separation in 1913 from his second wife, Maybelle, who returned to the United States with their two children. Now he threw himself 'even more into the hectic social whirl of an elegant man-about-town, famous for his numerous feminine conquests'.[9] And it was through this penchant for fashionable dalliances that – after Poiret, Doucet and Paquin – he met Gabrielle Chanel. Their affair was to continue for four turbulent years before being cut short by Iribe's death from a heart attack in 1935, at the early age of 52, at La Pausa, Chanel's villa at Roquebrune Cap Martin.

'Iribe and Chanel', according to Iribe's biographers, 'shared a mutual passion for clothes and jewelry, but in their ideas and their approaches to life they differed diametrically. He loved colours, brocaded fabrics and sophisticated shapes, while

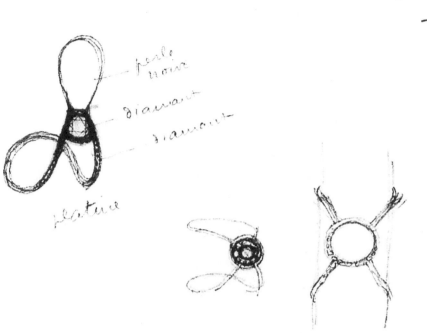

...ribe: page from a sketchbook,
study for rings,
1925/30.

she had brought into fashion the black dress, tweeds and the sporty look. . . . She was devoted to her work, while he, in his own inimitable fashion of course, was tremendously idle. He loved the social whirl and going out, while she made it a point of honour to refuse invitations.'[10] The dynamics of their affair were also a matter of power and self-image; Chanel has herself hinted as much, albeit obliquely: 'The most complex man I have ever known was Paul Iribe. He used to criticize me for not being straightforward. . . . Iribe loved me . . . while secretly hoping to destroy me. He wanted to see me conquered, humiliated, he wanted me to die. He would have felt a profound delight in seeing me entirely dependent on him, poor, reduced to powerlessness, paralysed in an invalid carriage. He was an extremely perverse person, highly affectionate, highly intelligent, highly interested, extraordinarily sophisticated. He was a Basque of astonishing moral and aesthetic versatility, but in his jealousy he was a true Spaniard.'[11]

Yet this marriage of opposites, this affectionate acrimony, was to produce among other things a superb collection which stands as Chanel's most remarkable work in the field of jewelry.

From 1 to 15 November 1932, under the aegis of Chanel, there took place in the private rooms at 29 Rue du Faubourg-Saint-Honoré an exhibition of sumptuous diamond jewelry. The brilliance of the stones was echoed by a glittering, luminous décor of crystal and mirror-glass, multiplied to infinity by the play of reflections. A series of photographs by André Kertész still bears witness to the magical charm of the setting: on black marble columns are arranged wax mannequins whose surreal delicacy serves as a backdrop to necklaces, brooches, ribbons and diadems. The jewelry was remarkable for the delicacy of its settings – with neither a clasp nor a mount to be seen – and was based on variations on three themes: bows, stars and feathers. There were also variations in function, each piece being designed to be worn in a number of different ways, with necklaces coming apart to make brooches, and bracelets and pendants becoming diadems.

Delicate strips of diamonds, as if made up of thousands of tiny flashes of light or beads of water, were only one example of the influence of Iribe, everywhere present at the exhibition. His contribution generally was beginning to be seen as of definitive importance in the shaping of the vision of the age: 'How great was Paul Iribe's influence on contemporary decorative art, and especially on jewelry! . . . Neither considerations of cost, nor technical difficulties, nor the accustomed habits of his clients could deter him. He was convinced, moreover, that none of these factors should be allowed to compromise the success of his jewelry if it found favour, as he believed that it corresponded to new fashions in jewelry. . . . Diamonds were no longer merely round, oval or rectangular as they used to be. Now they were cut in all shapes

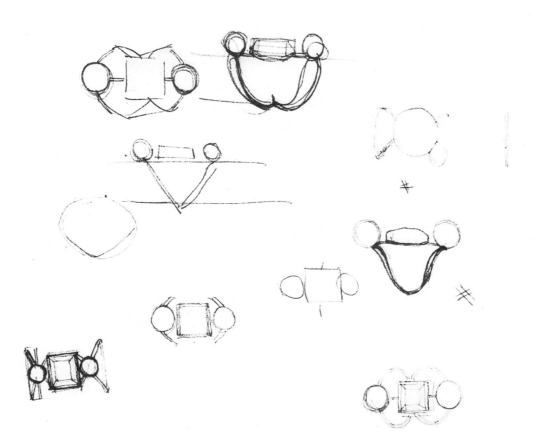

Iribe: page from a sketchbook,
study for rings,
1925/30.

and sizes, creating effects that were original and bizarre, with lines, triangles, hexagons, even trapezoids . . . '.[12]

A special brochure, printed by Draeger and containing five photographs by Robert Bresson and a short text by Chanel, was published to accompany the exhibition, and served only to underline the affinity of its vision and means of expression with those of Iribe, whose books it so closely resembled. We shall return to the content of the text when we come to discuss the *principles* of Chanel's aesthetic in the field of jewelry.

For both partners (and as is abundantly demonstrated by the many similar brochures produced by Iribe on other themes), what mattered above all was the assertion of a demand for total, absolute luxury. It was a luxury which, as will later be seen, was the product of the skill and virtuosity of the craftsman, of an extraordinary technical skill which owed nothing either to mechanization or to mass production. And this skill was in turn simply the reflection of a tradition perpetuated in local memory, which had now come to take root in a 'Frenchness' of which Iribe was the bard ('The Rue de la Paix is the expression of Paris, of ingenious, luxurious, inventive, creative Paris. . . . From the traditions of French fine art to the creations springing out of the fashion houses . . . a gentle current has begun to flow, lapping at Mansart's noble mansions on the Place Vendôme and bathing their façades, behind which the most inventive minds have at their disposal the wittiest fingers on earth,' he wrote in 1934 in his monograph *Vitrine de la France*).

The magnificence of the jewelry in the exhibition took Paris by storm, against an economic background that was fairly depressed, moreover. This was precisely the point Chanel chose to emphasize in her elegantly provocative exploration of her approach:

'The most diverse methods are quite legitimate in the profession that I exercise, provided that they are used only to follow fashion in its true direction. The reason which prompted me to want to design fake jewelry in the first place was that to me it seemed bereft of arrogance in an age of rather facile splendour. This consideration becomes less urgent at a time of financial crisis, when in every aspect of life there reappears an instinctive craving for authenticity, which reduces amusing imitations to their true worth.

'My reason for choosing diamonds is that, dense as they are, they represent the greatest worth in the smallest volume. And I have taken advantage of my fondness for all that glitters to attempt through jewelry to effect a reconciliation between elegance and fashion.'

In presenting diamonds as a symbol of authenticity Chanel wished to emphasize above all their clarity, their brilliance, their dimensions and what might be described as their transparent heaviness. For she chose to treat the stones in a manner which was the exact opposite of the usual approach, that is as tiny specks requiring huge settings, and to celebrate the stones as such, by contrast, presenting them without any

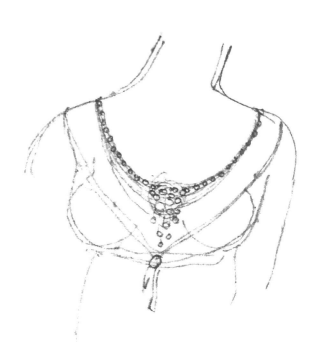

perles..
grand collier..
articulé
avec poignée
de perles et chute.

Iribe: page from a sketchbook,
study for a necklace,
1925/30.

visible settings at all. One ring, for example, is made out of two large square diamonds, with a setting consisting of only the bare minimum required to support them. The entire exhibition was intended as a celebration of precious stones in their purest form, of the qualities that render them a pure refraction of light.[13] There was also a specific contrast intended (though this has tended to be overlooked with the passing of time) with the nuances of emeralds, of which Paris was the centre of world trade and which were then enjoying great popularity with the public.

Sumptuousness at its most flagrant – the exhibition represented an outlay of 93 million francs at the time (a sum which led incidentally to the cancellation of the proposed transfer to London, because of the deposit, calculated as a proportion of the overall value, demanded by British customs) – was thus the principal reason for choosing diamonds. Even if it meant forsaking the world of the imagination for a more sober approach, Chanel seemed to be saying, let us do it without hesitation, let us go from one extreme to the other, for otherwise the whole approach loses its point.

Chanel would not allow herself to be confined by any orthodoxy, however, whatever it might be, nor would she let herself be limited to a display of splendour pure and simple. Thus she was careful to lay stress on the original aspects of her approach and the wholly contemporary rationale behind it. By making designs that moved, glided and flowed, she wanted her jewelry 'to be like ribbons on women's fingers. My jewelry is adaptable and can be dismantled and put back together again.

For grand occasions the whole composition can be worn. For more informal ones the central portion can be removed along with the larger sections. The set can be split up and parts of it worn on fabrics or furs. Thus a set of jewelry is no longer something immutable. Life transforms it, adapting it to its necessities. .

'This jewelry has left behind the puzzles, so literary as to have lost all plastic qualities, that the cubist vogue attempted to launch. I have sought out the shapes which best display the brilliance of diamonds to its best advantage – stars, crosses, drops in descending order of size, and great sparkling cabochons. That is the reason why I am presenting this jewelry not in caskets but on wax mannequins. These are not, it is important to remember, those stylized caricatures with which fashion – destined for women of flesh and blood – has nothing whatever to do. My waxen women are as close as possible to reality, like *photographs*. Some of my necklaces, following the shape of the neck, do not close; some of my rings coil up. Some of my bracelets drop the length of the arm, moulding themselves to its curve. My jewelry never stands in *isolation* from the idea of women and their dress. And because dresses change, so does my jewelry.'[14]

Unswervingly faithful to her principles, Chanel was unable to view her jewelry differently, as can be seen, or to divorce it from her fashion designs as a whole: the same concern for freedom and for flexibility, the same desire to follow the lines of the body that governed her clothes, also held good for her jewelry. And to this was added

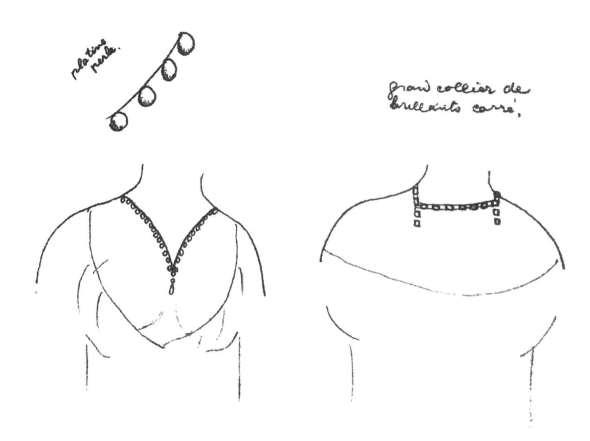

Iribe: page from a sketchbook,
study for necklaces,
1925/30.

that note of lyricism which is like Chanel's personal stamp, shaping a mythology and a set of themes of her own invention:

'In the past jewelry used to be *first and foremost* a matter of design. . . . My jewelry represents *first and foremost* an idea! . . . I wanted to cover women with constellations. With stars! Stars of all shapes and sizes to sparkle in their hair, tassels and crescent moons. See these comets, their heads resting on a woman's shoulder, their shimmering tails slipping behind the shoulders to fall in a shower of stars on the breast . . .'.[15]

Part Two

The years that Chanel spent with Iribe were also the time when she got to know Jean Cocteau, a friendship which was to last until his death in 1963. Cocteau had first met Iribe in 1909, at the first production of the lavish revue *Schéhérazade*, and had subsequently written the text of *Nijinski* and collaborated with him on *Le Témoin*. He had many friends in common with Iribe and Chanel, including Misia Sert, and it seemed inevitable that the writer and the admirer of Reverdy, Picasso and Stravinsky should work together. The opportunity presented itself in 1925, with the designs for *Le Train bleu* for Diaghilev, and twelve years later Chanel designed the costumes for *Les Chevaliers de la table ronde* and *Oedipe Roi*.

The 1932 exhibition, in a nutshell, had aimed straight at the essentials: with its costliness, its sophistication and its 'classic' minimalism, it was as though Chanel was determined early on to demonstrate her mastery of the field by setting her sights from the outset on its most challenging areas, while at the same time allowing her imagination to run free.

Numerous drawings by Cocteau, found in an envelope marked 'Chanel' that has recently been discovered, bear witness to the scale of the innovations in jewelry design on which she was intending to venture. The precious stones are used in a lyrical, magical fashion, in a series of unexpected metaphors, shifts of meaning and allusions, which was to be seen again later in Chanel's work with Fulco di Verdura.

Jean Cocteau: drawing from an unpublished portfolio, *c.* 1933.

Cocteau's drawings show suggested ideas for different ensembles like so many miniature scenarios, and it is impossible to know at this distance in time whether these grew out of discussions between the two interested parties or were the result of instructions given by Chanel to Cocteau. Thus a black velvet riding habit for evening wear is put together with a diamond-encrusted boater; we can picture breastplates in gold or gleaming silver 'moulded to the form of the breasts and stomach like those which used to be worn by men'; an officer's greatcoat is topped by a sort of Phrygian cap encircled by a golden laurel wreath; another overcoat in 'stone-grey material' is embellished with a diamond lizard; and a variety of other breastplates in gold and silver and circlets of beaten gold punctuate this series of drawings, which occupy the territory somewhere between fashion and theatre design. The theme that runs through them all is that of the warrior-queen, of an Antigone figure born of the ideal of Greece that was of such central importance to the personal mythology of the author of *Orphée*.

It was a theme to which Chanel was to return in 1937, when she helped with the design of Cocteau's *Oedipe Roi*, which highlighted two essential elements which were to become leitmotivs of Chanel's jewelry. Firstly there was the direct link that she established between jewelry and the theatre, by which jewelry was expected (like perfume moreover) to be distinguished by its absolute freedom, its luxuriance, its sophistication and its profusion. In this it was also required to function as a

Jean Cocteau: drawing from an unpublished portfolio, *c.* 1933.

28

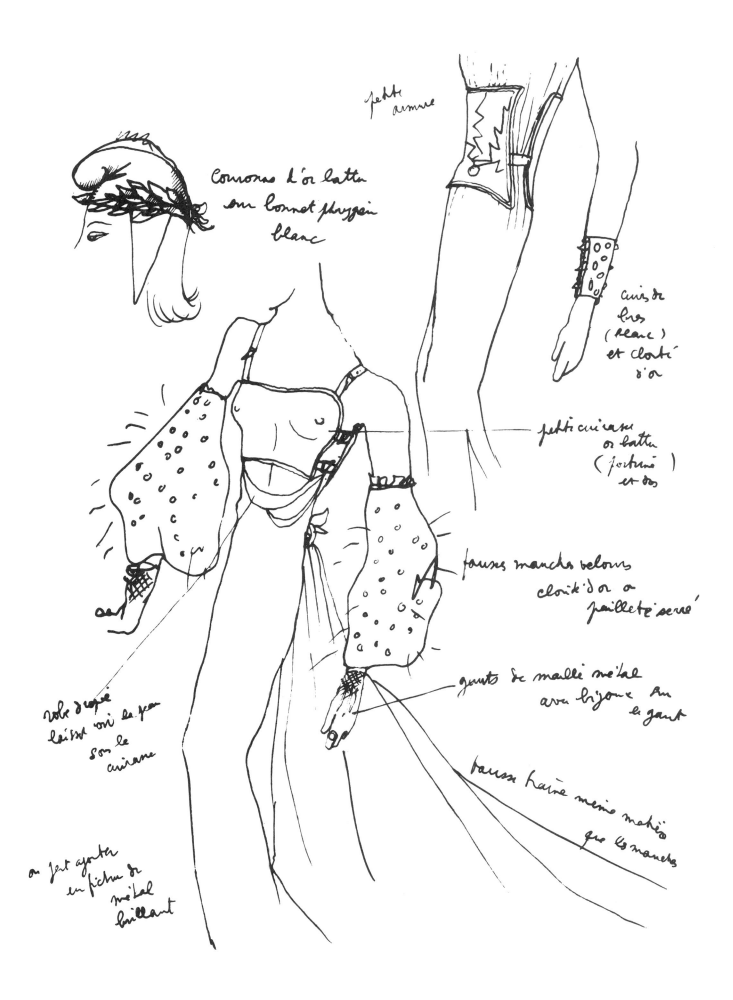

counterpoint to the severity of the cut and fabric of the clothes with which it was worn. This sophisticated theatricality was to be strengthened by her links with artists such as Picasso and Dalí, and above all by the tastes and interpretations of her new collaborators after the death of Iribe.

In the second place, these constant references to an archaic, classical Greece, to a mythical, primordial land, at once wild and symbolic, reflected a desire for an element of crude primitivism in Chanel's ineffably sophisticated designs for every piece: in contrast, she used to say, to 'Rue de la Paix' jewelry, jewelry-as-investment, jewelry-as-status-symbol, distinguished by the single characteristic of 'not being barbaric enough'. Thus she kept at a safe distance all the stuffiness, all the respectability of the period, banishing the entire spectrum of affectation, pretentiousness, codified elegance and smug triteness. Furthermore, the vogue for primitivism was one of the new movements then conquering the artistic élite among whom Chanel moved; she was following the trend of a generation which had turned its back on figurative art, on the obsession with acquiring technique, on concern about painting properly, on an entire venerable academic tradition, in order to embrace the whole gamut of art forms that had hitherto been shunned by the artistic establishment, from the images of Byzantine art to carvings from Africa. A child of her times, she had acquired the ability

Jean Cocteau: drawing from an unpublished portfolio, c. 1933.

to discern expressions of the utmost sophistication in the most seemingly naive or popular art forms.

She was confirmed in this view, according to her own account, by a visit she made to the imperial treasures and cabinets of curiosities in Vienna and Munich, the memory of which she never ceased to evoke throughout her career. Claudette Joannis has detected echoes of these ancient shapes and techniques in Chanel's work: 'In front of these pendants and brooches, how is it possible not to be reminded of those eighth-century silver fibulae with their heavy cabochons set in filigree surrounds, or of the Bavarian crown worn by the Empress Kunigunde in the eleventh century? In this treasure, as in the crown of Charlemagne, pearls, rubies and amethysts are arranged to form circles and squares.'[16] Another sign or symptom of 'barbarism', which was also to become a leitmotiv in Chanel's work throughout her career, was the setting of stones in cabochons carved in relief, so that the slight unevenness of the setting formed a contrast with the limpid transparency of the stones.

It was also at this time that distinguished art-lovers such as Georges Duthuit, son-in-law of Matisse, began to adopt a new approach to Byzantine art, of which Chanel had had some experience through a visit to the Tomb of Galla Placidia in Ravenna. Its influence can be seen especially clearly in the great number of crosses, with or without pendants, which she designed using combinations of pearls and precious stones. 'As for her long chains with pearls set in cones of delicately wrought metal,'

en 1937 - Robe du soir

Jean Cocteau
1937

Jean Cocteau: Coco Chanel,
drawing, 1937.

adds Joannis, 'here the influence is clearly more from the Renaissance; the drop pearls,
meanwhile, owe their inspiration to the age of the Baroque.'

For Chanel it was naturally not a matter of reconstruction pure and simple: she
was always intelligent enough to acknowledge that it is not possible to create out of
a void, but only by emulating the past. She would thus reinterpret existing models,
sometimes seeking advice from her chosen circle. Apart from Iribe, this also included
Etienne de Beaumont, famous for having been the model for Raymond Radiguet's
Comte d'Orgel (as well as, according to his own account, for Marcel Proust's Saint
Loup). To him, it seems, fell the key role of adviser on Chanel's jewelry from 1924. A
society figure *par excellence*, renowned for the sophistication of his tastes and the
magnificence of the balls he gave (and from which he always contrived to exclude
anyone who was not to his liking), he was essentially one of those artists (or masters
of the ephemeral) whom Chanel made a point of encouraging and fostering, if only
financially, throughout her life.

After the severity and economy of means, symbolic of 'French taste' as interpreted
by Iribe, Etienne de Beaumont's contribution was to lie more in the realms of
imagination, charm and dreamlike metaphors, which surrealism was to exploit to the
full in the fields of literature and the graphic arts, and whose subtle tonalities were

later to characterize Chanel's jewelry (de Beaumont was to design long chains embellished with irregularly shaped stones and coloured crosses, for example, reminiscent of those which Chanel received from the Grand Duke Dimitri).

Two other characters newly appeared on the scene were also to play a contributory part in this development. Faithful to her principle of plucking her collaborators from other, unconnected, fields, in response to what she saw as their true talents, Chanel asked François Hugo, then manager of her hosiery factory, to work with her on some of her jewelry; he was destined to become a goldsmith. She also, and perhaps most significantly, asked a young Sicilian aristocrat, whom she had engaged initially as a fabric designer, to turn his hand to jewelry. For six years from 1927 he was to work with Mademoiselle Chanel on a regular basis.

Fulco Santo Stefano della Cerda, Duke of Verdura, had been born in Palermo in 1898 into a famously eccentric family, and from his earliest childhood his tastes were strongly influenced by the flora and fauna of the Baroque era, not to speak of the architecture of Sicily, all of which was destined to marry so perfectly with Chanel's own tastes. From the dogs, cats, monkeys, mongooses, statues of dwarfs and giants, stucco saints and figures of little Negro boys in painted wood that surrounded him, they were together to derive a whole alphabet of shapes and designs, which were

Eric: Mlle Chanel, drawing,
Vogue, 1934.

later to appear in the necklaces and bracelets signed by Chanel, before he opened his own shop in New York.

Accounts of how the two of them met differ. After the death of his father in 1919, Verdura, then only nineteen years old, threw himself furiously into the café-society of the time, moving between Cannes, Venice and Paris. According to one story, it was during a trip to Venice, at one of the celebrated parties given by Linda and Cole Porter at the Palazzo Rezzonico, that he got to know the Porters and was encouraged by them to launch into fashion. Another, more romantic, version has it that he squandered what remained of his inheritance on a week-long party in Sicily and a ball on the theme of Lady Hamilton, from which he emerged to go immediately to Paris to work for Chanel (*The New Yorker*, May 1941, 13).

From Chanel, according to Diana Scarisbrick, he was to learn that 'there was more to the art [of jewelry] than cascades of blue-white diamonds in austere platinum settings; that an antique ruby or emerald cross might be pinned on the lapel of a tweed suit to devastating effect; and that proportion was the secret of good design. Chanel and Verdura had much in common: both despised the vulgarity of huge solitaires set in rings ("One might just as well tie a cheque around one's neck"), and both shunned the meagre and the insignificant. Verdura's designs [for Chanel] never centred around single stones; rather, he used his encyclopaedic knowledge of art history in adapting classical designs to modern tastes.'[17]

In all this he was remaining true to Chanel's guiding principle: her way of rewriting history, and of finding inspiration in the reinvention of ancient forms. This partnership was to produce above all else one of the pieces which has become emblematic of Chanel's jewelry of this period; a bracelet in enamel and precious stones bearing a Maltese cross, a motif that was deeply rooted in the Mediterranean culture of the young Sicilian, and which could not have failed to evoke in Chanel memories of a childhood spent within the walls of a convent and punctuated by this symbol, which she would never cease to use in her designs. A series of photographs taken at this time shows the two of them bending over one of these bracelets, moreover. The intense brilliance of the stones, arranged like a stained-glass window within the rough geometry of the design, contrasts with the still, matt whiteness of the enamel. These bracelets, which exist in a number of different versions, marked the revival of a hitherto forgotten technique, often to be repeated in Chanel's work: the laying down of successive layers of enamel and lacquer so as to impart subtle nuances to the base material, still visible through the different layers (in this case the gold of the bracelet can be discerned through the layers of enamel). This was a theme which was to recur in her later work. Again, it is the outward appearance, the face value of a precious material, which is denied, masked and stripped of all its conventional connotations.

Verdura was to execute a number of variations on the theme of the Maltese cross for Chanel, laying stress from 1930 onwards on the medieval or 'barbaric' associations

which were to assume such central importance in the imagery of the house of Chanel after the interruption of the war years. But Verdura's collaboration with the Rue Cambon was to be cut short when in 1934 he decided to follow his friend Baron Nicolas de Gunzburg, a prominent society figure, to New York. There he started out by designing for the jeweller Paul Flato, for whom in 1937 he opened a shop in Los Angeles which was to attract an enviable clientele of actresses and celebrities from the movie business. Returning to New York two years later, Verdura eventually started his own business, which enjoyed a success that was to continue for the next thirty years. His collaboration with Chanel was to prove of equal significance to both of them, however, based as it was around a handful of common themes; a taste for the Baroque and for uneven shapes, a freedom in the choice of the materials and the way they were put together (Verdura used to boast that he could transform an ordinary shell into a precious stone), an indifference to classic criteria of taste, a combination of extreme sophistication with primitivism, and finally a taste for unbridled luxury, distinguished by its gratuitousness and its unchallenged and total supremacy.

From 1924 onwards, Chanel entrusted the making of her jewelry to the firm of Gripoix, one of the foremost workshops in Paris. Gripoix were also responsible for perfecting a secret process by which molten glass, after being put through various

different treatments, was made to take on a pearly sheen, which meant that it could be used on details of every kind, from buttons to brooches and earrings. It was the Gripoix workshops, in addition, which adapted a number of these designs for costume jewelry, and which saw to the manufacturing side of a great deal of jewelry before the war years, when the fashion house was closed. This work is distinguished by the delicacy of its design – in contrast, frequently, to the cherished crudeness of the Byzantine and Russian designs – by its motifs of flowers, fruit or birds, and by its use of highly sophisticated enamelwork.

At the same time Chanel was developing a quite remarkable range of imagery in which the power of imagination reigned supreme. It was a 'fantasy' world, in the eighteenth-century sense of the expression, when it was used to describe landscapes or architecture: a world of dreams, that is to say, woven out of echoes and allusions, oscillating between the elegiac and a knowing irony. Colour, movement, allusiveness and a quality of bizarreness were the underlying principles of this aesthetic, which was shared simultaneously by Jean Schlumberger ('Even at this stage Schlumberger enjoyed strange organic themes, the compelling curiosities of nature. He was also fascinated by allegorical jewels, and by the rich and timeless pageantry of ritual and theatre.')[18] This was the time when people were rediscovering the outmoded charms of Napoleon III cherubs, of Dresden china flowers, of little Negro boys and bunches of bigarreau cherries in Venetian glass; when Christian Bérard was giving free rein to his imagination; when there was a vogue for masquerades and fancy-dress balls and for a sensuality that grew in intensity as it became concentrated on fabrics and precious stones; the time, in short, when all these factors combined to dispel any lingering shadows of misplaced austerity or puritanism.

Chanel created earrings in the form of parchment scrolls, evoking the illusory quality of stucco panels, and proposed a *trompe l'oeil* medal; she made use of an ingenious exoticism, taking up the palm-tree motif which Schlumberger also used and adding a little Mexican, and creating a 'Picadilly' brooch as an ironic symbol of her well-known anglophilia. Schiaparelli had taken up the motif of the heart pierced by swords, so dear to Neapolitan culture (Cecil Beaton had also suggested the design of a heart pierced by a rose with a long golden stem, from which would fall drops made of rubies); Chanel chose to base her interpretation on the more popular version of the motif, adding a further twist to her sophistication by applying it to a naive and outdated symbol of sentimentality. This playful, 'fantasy' imagery thus appeared as another reverberation of that passion for the strange and dreamlike which Chanel encountered in most of the painters whom she encouraged or in whose circles she mixed.

Chanel used to employ the services of the goldsmith De Gorse, whose remarkable mastery of his craft she held in high regard. When she wanted to resume production after the interruption of the war years she naturally turned again to De Gorse, quite undeterred by the fact that he had meanwhile closed down his business. Thus it was that, through De Gorse's intervention, Robert Goossens, then only twenty-seven years old, began working for Chanel in a rather roundabout fashion in 1954. He did not actually meet her until the death of De Gorse, six years later. The son of a foundry-worker, he had been discouraged by his father from following him into that dangerous trade. His work was primarily in the finest materials, that is gold and silver, since making what was then fantasy jewelry – before becoming today's designer jewelry – was deemed hardly worthy of consideration in those days.

Chanel's working methods, recalls Robert Goossens, were the same for her jewelry as for her clothes: working directly with the material, without any preconceived notions, she would drape the fabric straight over the model or would model shapes in some malleable material. Marcel Haedrich describes the scene: 'To make her jewelry she would sit in her salon, perched on the edge of the sofa and playing with a ball of soft plastic, like chewing gum. In front of her, on the very low Chinese table, there would be boxes and little bowls holding stones of all different shapes and sizes which she would embed in her gum, flattened out on the table, as the fancy took her. She would use either genuine or imitation stones, taking into account only their overall effect in the design. She possessed magnificent emeralds and the loveliest and rarest rubies, but she was just as fond of pink Siamese rubies and pale sapphires from Ceylon, which were of no great value, and topazes. "There is nothing prettier", she used to say, "than the gilded waters of a topaz." '[19]

There still exist some of these arrangements of stones set in plastic, like bizarre reliquaries, which could be rearranged *ad infinitum*, according to the occasion and the needs of the moment. Chanel would indicate the way the stones should be arranged on the metal base. There were also, most importantly, the innumerable books which Mademoiselle would thrust under the young goldsmith's nose for him to find the required reference. Great tomes on the *The Enamels of Georgia* or *Antique Jewelry* are still to be found on the shelves of his workshop. Chanel did not rule out the use of direct quotations of ancient forms, which always appear like a shorthand for her own dazzlement, as a heartfelt tribute and a record of her encounters with memorable objects. Another aspect of her rebuttal of traditional canons of taste where jewelry was concerned was her habit of considering rings or necklaces first and foremost as genuine art objects, as creations with their own logic and as intimations of absolute beauty, and not as financial *tours de force*. Her passion for jewelry was thus shot through with memories and evocations of visits to museums and galleries filled with the glitter of exceptional pieces. We have already seen the significance that her visit to the Schatzkammer at Munich had for her, crystallizing as

it did her taste for rugged forms and impressive stones, and she also went several times (with Misia Sert in particular) to the Treasury of St Mark's in Venice, with its onyx, agate and chalcedony goblets from the eleventh century, its Byzantine glasses, its alabaster paterae and its tenth-century rock crystals, its enamels set in gold filigree and an enormous bezel ring. She also used to go frequently to the galleries of ancient art in the Louvre, where it is easy to imagine her stopping short in front of a solid gold bracelet studded with emeralds and rubies which belonged to a Syrian princess of the third century and came from Yakmur: a heavy, irregularly cut band with a pitted surface, an object so crude as to defy any notions of elegance, and which conjures up a whole improbable era, a civilization in which violence was omnipresent. As testimony to the strength of its effect on Chanel we have an almost exact replica of this bracelet, made by Robert Goossens's workshops without his having any idea of the provenance of the design.

To her memories of these visits Chanel would also add the treasure-store of designs contained in a collection of precious objects which had survived the period of closure during the war: eighth-century fibulae, an eleventh-century Bavarian crown, long strings of irregularly shaped pearls from the Renaissance and so on. The Egyptians, Persians, Etruscans, Visigoths, Carolingians and Celts all served her purpose equally well, and it was the Egyptians who invented the idea of using *pâte de verre* and *pietra dura* together with the more traditional precious stones. Thus it was

that, shot through with allusions and transformed into a mosaic of traces and fragments, jewelry definitively shed its habitual connotations to enter the realms of art and of aesthetic pleasure.

Wanting finally to judge the effect of her jewelry, Chanel would try the finished pieces on models draped for the occasion in white smocks: emblems, relics or reliefs standing out in every detail against a blank page.

hristian Bérard: evening dress
by Chanel,
watercolour, 1937.

Part Three

'Out of my distress
I invented the little black dress'

So declares the heroine of the musical comedy in which Chanel saw herself immortalized in her own lifetime. And it is clear that Chanel will be remembered in the imagery of the twentieth century essentially for her aesthetic of severity, the gesture with which she swept away the stereotype of women that had been left over from the previous century. At the same time there is a tendency to forget that this sophisticated economy of cut and fabric was inseparable in Chanel's eyes from a complementary development in jewelry. The utter simplicity and discretion of the one were to be countered by the consummate excess and serene ostentatiousness of the other. It is not difficult to find a sociological justification for this line of reasoning: as wealth and luxury goods have become relatively more widely distributed, as social barriers have been broken down, and as standards of living have generally improved, so little by little the boundaries of taste, which used to be clearly established and upheld by tradition, began to shift, before disappearing entirely. Exhilarating and light-hearted at first, in the end this freedom became a negative force, to the extent that it no longer safeguarded feelings of belonging to a particular group, nor did it guarantee adherence to a hierarchy or system of values. In the wake of this process, which has continued to accelerate throughout the century, tailored suits and the little black dress have assumed the significance of fixed points, means of expressing oneself with dignity, of placing oneself out of reach of the possible pitfalls of changing tastes and among the ranks of a timeless, secular aristocracy.

Christian Bérard: Mlle Cha
in her apartment at the Ritz
drawing, *Vogue*, 1937.

In her own way Chanel was an example of this change in values: she started out within a class system which, in her own inimitable fashion, she flouted; having sprung from the lowest rungs of society, she proceeded to set herself up as interpreter of the highest. From being a simple observer on the margins of society, 'invited' or excluded, she rose to play a leading role, and finally, it could almost be said, to be the scriptwriter. Her fashion designs, categorized at first as 'easy to wear', finally came to be viewed as symbols of a (good) taste that she had the gift of being able to interpret. But from her original social 'shift', from the fact that with a single movement she had managed to cut across the entire spectrum of society, she always retained a fierce indifference to traditional conventions, and her aesthetic was continually influenced by her desire to cut herself off from them, to shift the rungs of the social ladder.

In the art of jewelry as in fashion, and in her entire approach to life, in fact, Chanel remained faithful to a single tenet, summed up in a celebrated phrase (*'luxury is not the opposite of poverty, it is the opposite of vulgarity'*); a principle which led her to utter the luminous declaration that 'jewelry should be viewed with innocence, with artlessness, just as we enjoy the sight of an apple tree in blossom at the side of the road as we speed past in a motor-car'.[20] (Without knowing it, she was reiterating Augustin de Saint-Aubin's eighteenth-century definition of precious objects, and of elegance in general, as things that should only be glimpsed fleetingly, as gesture and movement allow.)

ean Cocteau: drawing from
n unpublished portfolio,
c. 1933.

And in retracing the thread of incidents concerned with jewelry in Chanel's life, it becomes clear how constantly, as a deliberate strategy, she strove to divest her jewelry of its conventional value and to restore to it an 'innocence'. The 1932 exhibition, with its somewhat sober forms, its exceptional stones, its undetectable settings and its enormously high prices, mounted at a time of crisis, seemed to be making a statement against assuming a discreet or subdued appearance in such circumstances, while she subsequently took a provocative delight in opposing parodies of imitation to self-satisfied opulence, and fake jewelry to pretentiousness.

It also becomes clear how Chanel's tastes developed to the point where she could exclaim finally: 'Why does everything I do turn out Byzantine?' From purity of outline to the Baroque, her tastes turned ever more exclusively towards massive, irregular pieces, the very opposite of any notion of prettiness – as favoured by classic jewelry – of a revived primitivism which she favoured from the middle of the century. Two characteristics distinguish this jewelry, which will always be of particularly special significance as the ultimate expression of Chanel's aesthetic: its dimensions, its relatively excessive and in one sense 'indiscreet' bulk, and the deliberate irregularity of its manufacture, a sophisticated crudeness in its execution. And these characteristics are precisely those over which the battle between the 'genuine' and the 'fake', between real jewelry and imitation jewelry, traditionally rages. ('When you make imitation jewelry you always make it bigger.')[21]

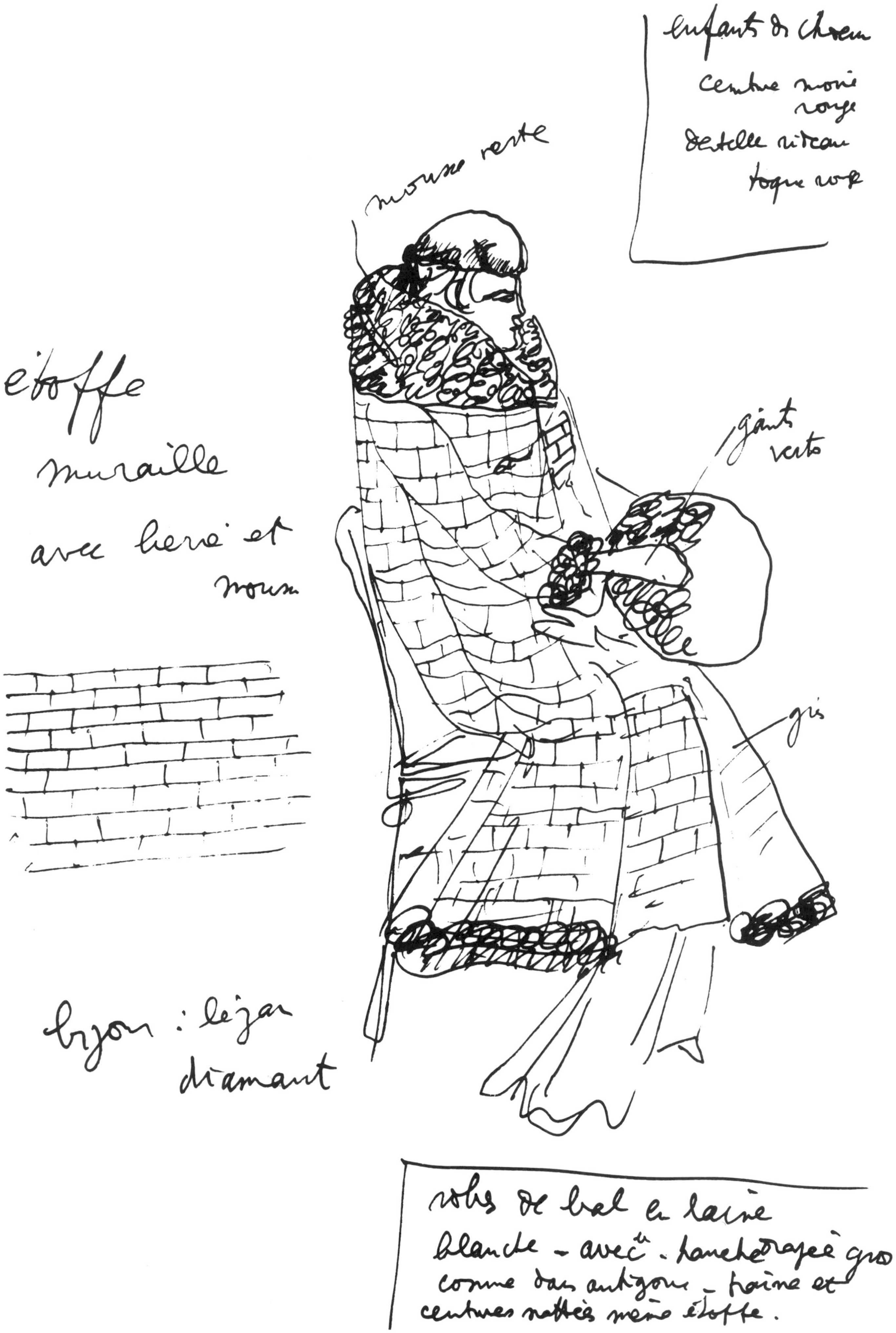

This opposition is clearly of central importance for any study of Chanel, credited as she is by tradition (and caricature) with the invention and consecration of the concept of 'designer' jewelry to the detriment of traditional jewelry, each of these categories being held to be exclusive of the other. This is a wholesale misinterpretation which should be rectified, if only by means of an exploration, like Georg Simmel's in a famous chapter on adornment in his *Soziologie*, of the wholly different functions of these two different types of object. Imitation or designer jewels, he concludes, justify themselves through 'what they momentarily *do* for their wearer; genuine jewels are a value that goes beyond this: they have their roots in the value ideas of the whole social circle and are ramified through all of it. Thus, the charm and the accent they give the individual who wears them feed on this super-individual soil. Their genuineness makes their aesthetic value – which, too, is here a value "for the others" – a symbol of general esteem, and of membership in the total social value system.'[22]

The difference in effect stems from the inherent contradiction implied in the wearing of jewelry, and in the need we feel to adorn ourselves: 'One adorns oneself for oneself, but can do so only by adornment for others. It is one of the strangest sociological combinations that an act, which exclusively serves the emphasis and increased significance of the actor, nevertheless attains this goal just as exclusively in the pleasure, in the visual delight it offers to others, and in their gratitude.'[23]

Jean Cocteau: drawing from an unpublished portfolio, *c.* 1933.

Sensitive as she was to the minutest workings of the society that surrounded her, and of the circles, fashionable or otherwise, through which she moved, Chanel could not help but be aware, even if only in a vague sort of way, of this essential ambiguity inherent in jewelry, of this curious egoism which is at the same time undeniably altruistic. ('Adornment is the egoistic element as such: it singles out its wearer, whose self-feeling it embodies and increases at the cost of others. . . . But, at the same time, adornment is altruistic: its pleasure is designed for the others, since its owner can enjoy it only insofar as he mirrors himself in them; he renders the adornment valuable only through the reflection of this gift of his.')[24]

Because they possess something of the eternal, of the changeless, of the extravagant, because they are impervious to decay and the ravages of time, precious stones reflect an image of the person wearing them that is, in a manner of speaking, sublime. ('That this nature of stone and metal – solidly closed within itself, in no way alluding to any individuality; hard, unmodifiable – is yet forced to serve the person, this is its subtlest fascination.')[25] Costume jewelry, on the other hand, abolishes this gulf in order to establish a sort of collusion between the wearer and the observer, which depends, rather like theatre, on a sense of shared illusion, on a willingness to play by the rules of the game of imitation. ('The unauthentic,' writes Simmel, contrasting it with the genuine, 'is only what it can be taken for at the moment.')[26] It is not therefore difficult to understand Chanel's desire throughout her life to work on *both* levels,

Christian Bérard: portrait
of Chanel,
charcoal on paper, 1926.

frequently intermingling the second (costume jewelry) with the first (the genuine article), the better to celebrate them in their respective functions.

Herein lies a perfectionism, an unswerving insistence on principles, that is illustrated by so many anecdotes about Chanel. Thus, when she makes the 'genuine' jewel the subject of a secret liturgy, a peculiar celebration of the intimate, her primary concern is to rescue it from misunderstanding and pretence, to free it from an exclusively social value in order to restore to it a purifying worth: that of inessentiality and superfluousness, of what (in Simmel's words) 'flows over', transcends the necessary requirements of life, and, in its very essence, is limitless and immaterial to the human condition. Here is a sovereignty which, on all the evidence, Chanel's whole being would sometimes seem to personify. 'This object subtly turned in on itself' . . . everything about her – the firmly drawn lines of her face, her ways of doing things, the very rhythm of her approach – seems to summon up a parallel (in the manner of the correspondences known in the Middle Ages as 'signatures', by which two distinct entities would demonstrate their common nature) with precious stones. The very fact that she railed so often, and with such feeling, speaking rapidly and in a brusque tone, against the simple investment value, the mercantile nature, imputed to costume jewelry, is enough to show by contrast the degree of importance that she accorded it, returning to the idea of a pure and simple delight in objects that are extremely small and ruinously expensive.

In the 'water' of a stone or the 'orient' of a pearl she clearly appreciated the interaction of form and colour, the virtuosity of the cut and the mount, the subtlety of the arrangement and the infinite play of the reflections; but she was also moved by that quality which perhaps above all sets the existence of a precious stone at the very opposite pole from that of a human being: its inconceivable transparency, and absolute changelessness. 'Solitaire' is a term (and like so many words it tells us much more than its apparent meaning) which is as central to the legend of Chanel as it is to the art of decorative jewelry. No doubt she found in it an echo of her own lofty supremacy, of her own fervent passion for beauty. Yes, the young girl who contemplated the austere crucifixes hanging on the walls of her convent, the unorthodox creature who accepted the Grand Duke Dimitri's necklace and the Duke of Westminster's emeralds, and who transformed the classicism of Iribe just as she did the mythological fantasies of a Cocteau or a Verdura – this woman who helped to revolutionize our conception of elegance found herself, as in so many symbols, in the dazzling flash of a diamond and the liquid gold of a topaz.

The Plates

CHANEL'S STYLE

Chanel's hands,
photographed by André Kertész,
c. 1938 (page 57).

Chanel on the balcony of her apartment
at the Ritz, Paris, in 1935.

Chanel photographed by Hoyningen-Huene,
1935.

Chanel's dressing table, 1937:
a shimmering expanse of silver, pearl
and mother-of-pearl.

Chanel in 1936.

Chanel in her apartment
at the Ritz, 1937.

Chanel with her accordion, 1937:
ivory stops, 'barbaric' bracelet,
emerald and diamond necklace.

Chanel in front of a portfolio
of wedding dresses, 1937.

Coco Chanel and Muriel Maxwell,
photographed by Horst, 1938.

Modèle de Monel ... Salon Chanel oct 1932

Modèle N° 630. —
Crêpe-satin.
Chanel.

vertès

Patchwork of fashion drawings, 1925/45:
Christian Bérard, Gabrielle Chanel,
Marcel Vertès, *et al.*

Chanel's hands,
photographed by François Kollar, 1937:
gold at her fingertips.

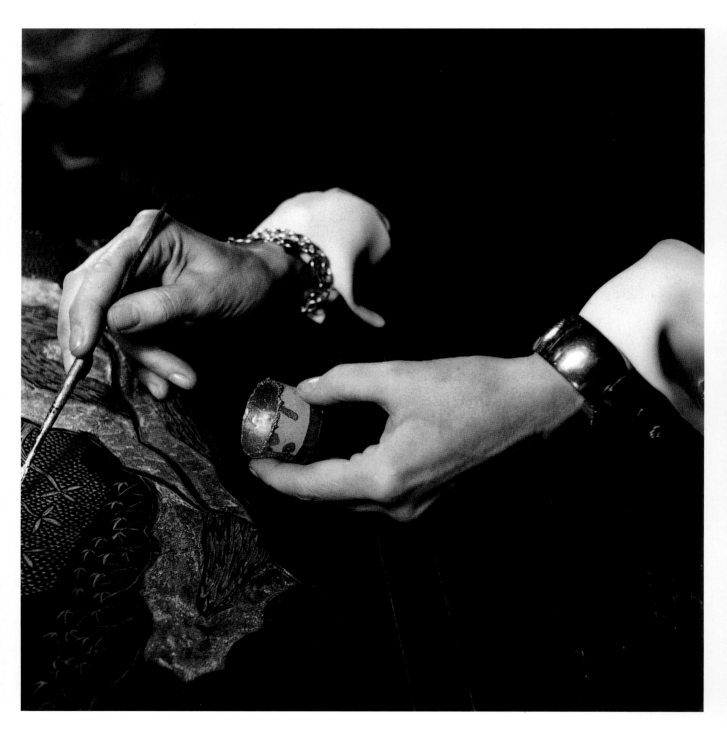

A SHOWER OF STARS

Diamond necklace and diadem on a wax mannequin,
Chanel, 1932.
With its sumptuousness, its elegance and its classic taste,
the *Bijoux de diamants* exhibition
held by Chanel in her Faubourg-Saint-Honoré *hôtel* in 1932
set out to conquer the prevailing gloom of the period.

Study for a necklace by Paul Iribe, *c.* 1925/30.

D iamond brooches and diadem shimmering like stars
on a wax mannequin, Chanel, 1932.

C hanel brooch, c. 1955.
The star has become a living creature.

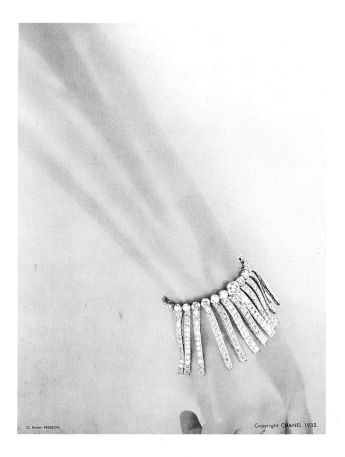

Diamond bracelet, Chanel, 1932. . . .
Fringes . . .

Diamond open necklace, Chanel, 1932.
. . . and a comet.

Illustration by Paul Iribe for the magazine *Choix*,
June 1930, showing use of
the comet theme.

Study for a necklace by Paul Iribe,
c. 1925/30.

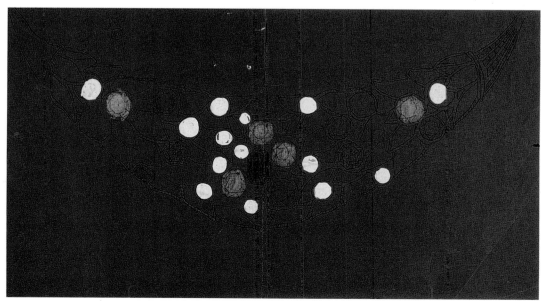

Diamond diadem, Chanel, 1932.

The sparkling scene at the 1932 exhibition
in the Rue du Faubourg-Saint-Honoré.
Baron Nicolas de Gunzburg, Princess J.-L. de Faucigny-Lucinge
and Mme Ralli admire the collection under the camera lens
of André Kertész.

Cl. Robert BRESSON.   Copyright CHANEL 1932.

Braids, bows and ribbons.

Diamond necklace, Chanel, 1932.

Headband, signed Chanel, c. 1960.

Headband, signed Chanel, c. 1960.

Landscapes of Fantasy

Wearing a large gold, amethyst and emerald ring,
Chanel takes a cigarette from a box
with a lid of rubies and white and blue sapphires.

Chanel, described by Paul Morand as
'*La belle dame sans merci*'.

Renaissance-inspired necklace,
sparkling with emeralds and topaz.

Bows and stylized flowers
form an elegant combination in a bracelet
of seventeenth-century inspiration.

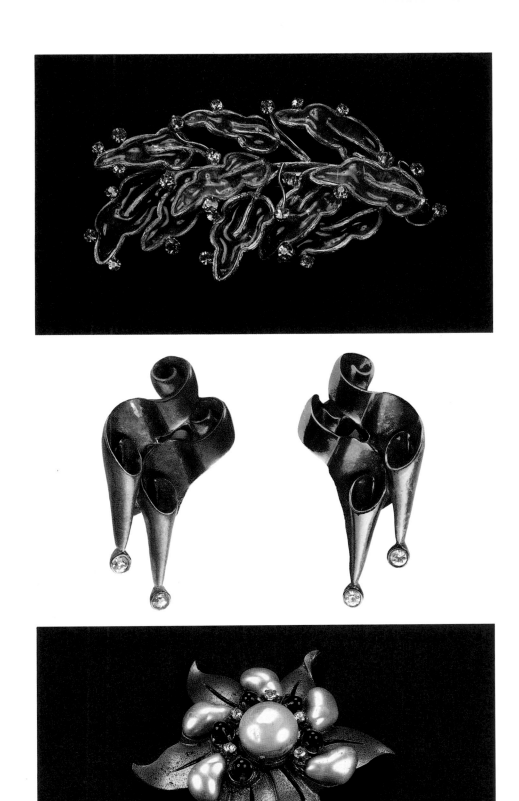

*L*eaf brooch, 1935/38.

*S*croll earrings.

*S*tylized Flower brooch, 1928/35.

Drawing by Giorgio de Chirico for a *Vogue* cover,
December 1935, showing jewelry by Chanel.
A rope of pearls is intertwined with a short garnet necklace
mounted on a twist of gold.

Bijoux de Fleurs

Chanel. Collier composé de glands et de
feuilles de chêne en émail transparent.

Chanel. Un bouquet de fleurs mélangées
fait un clip en émail multicolore et or.

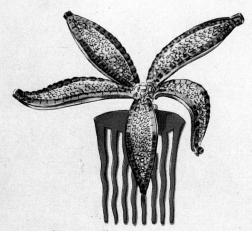

Paquin. Peigne pour le soir surmonté
d'une orchidée en similis bleus et blancs.

Chanel. Collier composé de pensées dégra-
dées, en émail, cœur rubis, feuilles vertes.

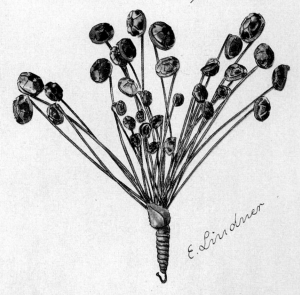

Schiaparelli. Le Comte E. de Beaumont
a créé ce clip en pierres fantaisie et émail.

Chanel. Broche faite de tiges dorées
s'épanouissant en pampilles multicolores.

Illustration from *Vogue*,
April 1938.
Bijoux de Fleurs (Flower Jewelry):
four pieces by Chanel,
one by Schiaparelli, one by Paquin.

Chanel necklace
on a wax mannequin, 1938.

Flower necklace.
The influence of natural forms,
always an underlying presence
throughout the history of jewelry,
had been particularly strong
in the mid-eighteenth century
and the years 1860–80,
and was to return in force in the 1940s.

*P*alm *Tree* brooch.

*T*rafalgar–*Picadilly* [*sic*] brooch.

'It had taken six years for Chanel to cross the road
from her office to the Ritz for lunch . . .
it was three hours before she was to re-emerge.'
Photograph by Hatami.

FRIENDSHIP WITH VERDURA

Coco Chanel and Fulco di Verdura in 1937.
Both embroidered on the theme of the Maltese cross,
creating an infinite number of variations
on its traditional eight points.

Two bracelets, *c.* 1960.

Two bracelets executed by Fulco di Verdura, *c.* 1937.

Brooch executed by Fulco di Verdura, 1925/32.

Coco Chanel wearing a Maltese cross bracelet,
gold and topaz ring, and gold-wire belt,
photographed by François Kollar, *c.* 1937.

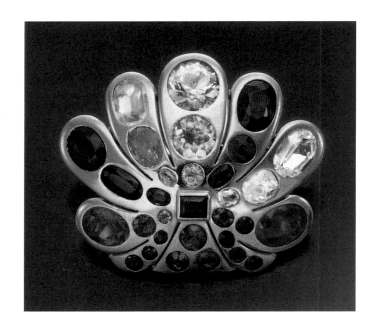

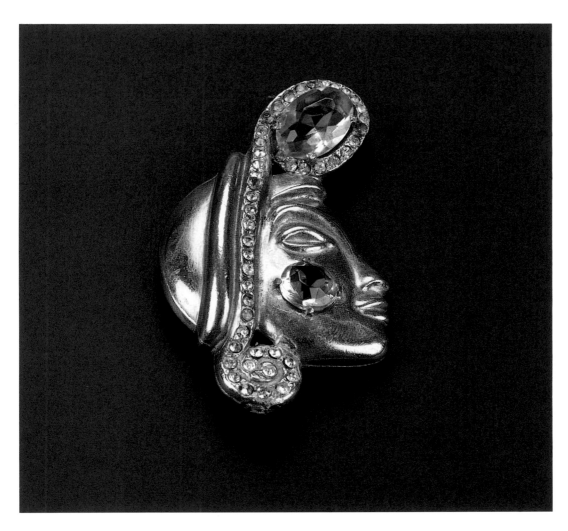

*E*ffigy brooch
executed by Fulco di Verdura,
signed Chanel, 1925/38.

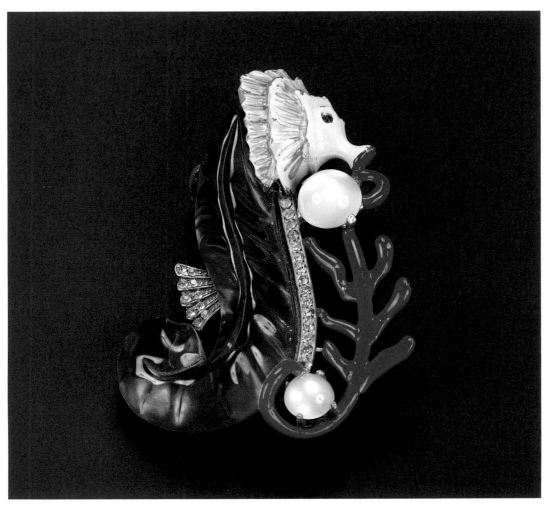

*S*ea-horse brooch
executed by Fulco di Verdura,
signed Chanel, 1933/38.

Rose brooch executed by Fulco di Verdura,
signed Chanel, 1935.
In diametric opposition to the tendency
towards geometrical forms then current,
here the naturalistic influence is seen
at its height.

AFTER THE WAR

Pendant cross on Chanel chain, 1954/71.
Chanel based all the crosses executed by Robert Goossens
on a cross given to her by a friend.

Twisted gold bracelet and cuff bracelet, Chanel, 1954/71.

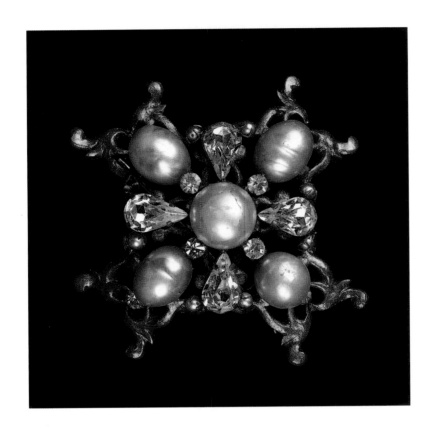

Variations on combinations of pearl and gold,
elegance and sobriety.

Earrings, bracelet and barrette,
Chanel, 1954/71.

Open-work brooch,
signed Chanel, 1954/71.

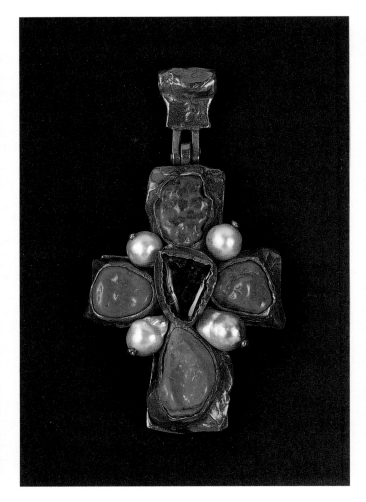

Turquoise sautoir and brooch, Chanel, 1954/71.

Gold, baroque pearl, turquoise and tourmaline cross
executed by Robert Goossens for Mlle Chanel,
with a saint in Byzantine style
engraved on the reverse, 1960s.

Brooch and necklace, Chanel, 1954/71.
The medieval influence is here subtly refined.

Gold cross engraved with a saint
in Byzantine style, 1954/71.

Cross of gold and four rock crystals, 1954/71.

Cross of gold and five rock crystals, 1954/71.

THE SPIRIT OF THE AGES

The influence of barbarism

Bracelet from Yakmur (Syria),
gold and stones, third century.

Bracelet executed by Robert Goossens
for Mlle Chanel, 1954/71.
The multicoloured cabochons set in broad,
raised incrustations are inspired by
the Yakmur bracelet in the Louvre.

Merovingian four-lobed fibula
from Humbécourt (Haute-Marne),
gold filigree and mounted stones,
eighth century.

Necklace of Byzantine inspiration, Chanel, 1954/71.

Chains and pearls: Chanel necklaces.

With her interpretations of the theme of the Maltese cross,
formerly worn by Grand Masters of the order hanging from a sumptuous cha[...]
its links woven through with rubies and sapphires,
Chanel created brooches and bracelets of an imperious beauty.

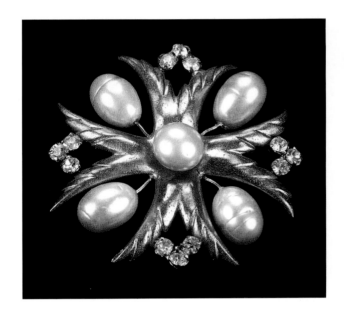

Cross of the Knights of Malta,
sixteenth century.

Brooch in the form
of a Maltese cross,
1928/35.

Chanel cuff bracelet
with Maltese cross
worn by Diana Vreeland,
c. 1950.

Coco Chanel at work,
photographed by Hatami.

Chanel's imagination was always fired by the st[u]dy of historical styles.

Anne of Cleves (detail)
by Hans Holbein the Younger, 1539,
showing jewelry in vogue
in the first half of the sixteenth century.

Byzantine clasp in the form of a Greek cross,
gold and precious stones, sixth century.

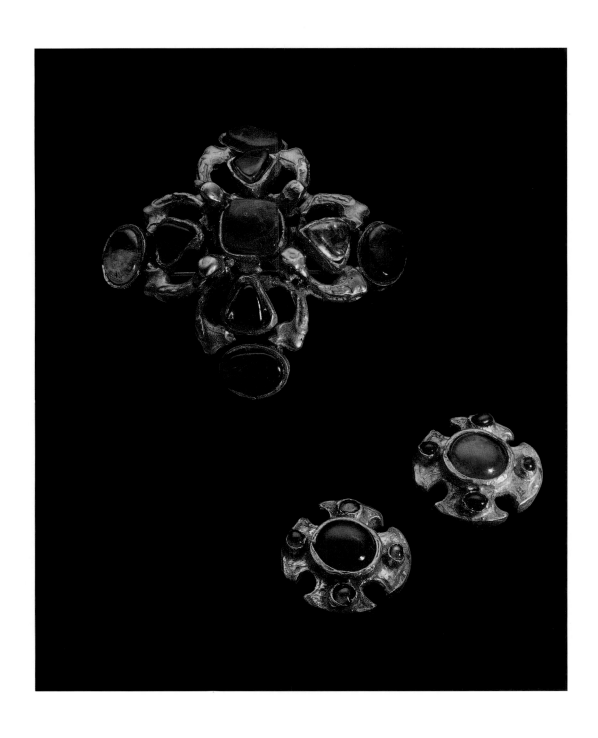

Brooch and earrings, Chanel, 1954/71.

Veronese's *Portrait of a Woman* (detail)
shows the sort of jewelry
in fashion in the sixteenth century,
age of a new refinement.

Chanel brooch, *c.* 1960.
This piece recalls Renaissance work
and its characteristic use of
open-work structures and faceted gems.

Articulated necklace
of Renaissance inspiration,
1930/40.

Two bracelets in the Renaissance manner. These unique pieces were Chanel's last creations before her death.

Rigid collar with interlacings of flowers and foliage executed by Robert Goossens, signed Chanel, c. 1960.

Belt of gilded fabric, Chanel, 1954/71. The elaboration of the design and the floral motif recall the fashions of the first half of the seventeenth century.

THE RUE CAMBON

Showcase of Chanel jewelry, 1937.

Photographs of Chanel's jewelry
by Hoyningen-Huene for *Harper's Bazaar*,
1 September 1960.

Frog and *Pierced Heart* brooches.

117

Chanel suit and jewelry, *Marie Claire*, September 1961.

Gleaming gold, mother-of-pearl and silver on Chanel earrings, brooches and necklaces, winter 1962.

Blue, white and gold 'plastron' necklace worn by Chanel.

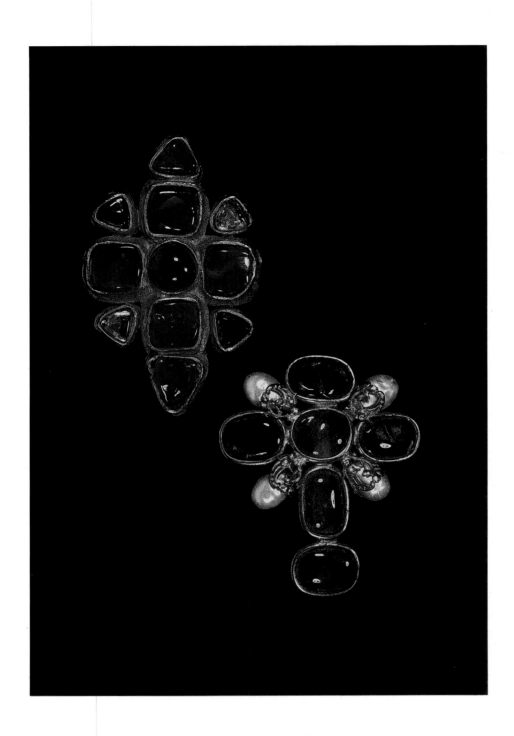

Two brooches of Byzantine inspiration
from Chanel's personal collection,
signed Chanel, *c.* 1960.

Filigree brooch, autumn–winter collection 1969.

Lion's-head pendant culminating
in thirty-four small chains,
executed by Desrues, 1955.

Brooch and necklace of Byzantine inspiration, 1966,
on a tweed suit that belonged to Coco Chanel.

Two crosses of Byzantine and Russian inspiration.
Chanel was fired with enthusiasm for Byzantine art
following a visit to the Tomb of Galla Placidia in Ravenna.

Brooch in the form of a cross, 1967,
on a silk crêpe jacket that belonged to Chanel.

Chanel necklace: geometric and floral motifs combined
in a firework display of dazzling colours.
Chanel necklace: sacred and profane combined.

CHANEL'S STYLE

Chanel in front of a portfolio of wedding dresses, 1937.

Chanel photographed by Horst, 1937.

Taking her inspiration from Indian jewelry,
of which she possessed some fine examples,
Chanel transformed the 'plastron' of this choker
into a plant-like rivière.

Chanel at the Ritz, *c.* 1938.

Day by day, the favourite necklace: gold, ruby and emerald.

Chanel and Jouvet, 1938.

Chanel in 1937.

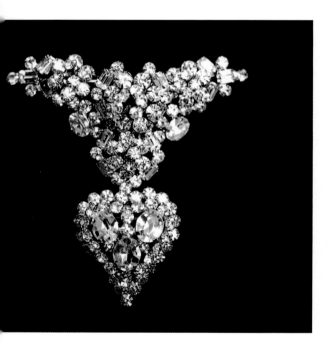

Chanel brooch:
'Jewelry for any time of the day or night,
sumptuous and generous.'
Marie Claire, March 1956.

C*oco Chanel* by Cassandre, 1940.

Chanel in 1957, on her way to Dallas
to receive a Fashion Oscar.

Brooch, c. 1955.
Emblematic of Chanel's style,
this piece marries the theme of the cross with floral motifs
and the sophisticated combination of pearls and gold.

Chanel photographed by Horst, c. 1960.

Chanel in her apartment at the Ritz, 1937 (page 136).

Notes to the Text
List of Illustrations
Bibliography
Index

Notes to the Text

1   Quoted by Claude Berthod, *Elle*, 8 November 1971.

2   Paul Morand, *L'Allure de Chanel*, Hermann, Paris 1976, p. 117.

3   Marcel Haedrich, *Coco Chanel*, Belfond, Paris 1987, p. 72.

4   Edmonde Charles-Roux, *Le Temps Chanel*, Chêne/Grasset, Paris 1988, p. 168.

5   Haedrich, *op. cit.*, pp. 66, 103.

6   *Ibid.*, p. 110.

7   Raymond Bachollet, Daniel Bordet, Anne-Claude Lelieur, *Paul Iribe*, Denoël, Paris 1982, pp. 85–9.

8   Quoted in *Paul Iribe*, exhibition catalogue, Bibliothèque Forney, Paris 1983, p. 79.

9   *Ibid.*, p. 119.

10   Bachollet *et al.*, *op. cit.*, p. 199.

11   Quoted by Morand, *op. cit.*, pp. 103–6.

12   Robert Linzeler, 'La Joaillerie française à l'exposition', *Vogue*, Paris, 1 September 1925, p. 31.

13   'Chanel's great innovation is in the displaying of diamonds unadorned, without any visible setting. Avoiding the use of small stones, slivers and splinters which have no true worth, Mlle Chanel has employed only stones of the finest quality and of medium size, which always keep their intrinsic value.' Marcel Astruc, *Les Annales*, 18 November 1932.

14   'Gabrielle Chanel nous parle', *L'Intransigeant*, 8 November 1932.

15   'Le luxe de Paris contre le chômage', *L'Intransigeant*, 26 October 1932.

16   *Chanel*, exhibition catalogue, Bunkamura, Tokyo 1990, pp. 74–5.

17   Diana Scarisbrick, *Departures*, American Express Incorporated, September/October 1989, p. 78.

18   Vivienne Becker, *Jean Schlumberger*, F.M.R., Milan 1991, p. 45.

19   Haedrich, *op. cit.*, pp. 223–4.

20   Morand, *op. cit.*, p. 117.

21   Haedrich, *op. cit.*, p. 222.

22   Georg Simmel, *Soziologie, Untersuchungen über die Formen der Vergesellschaftung*, Duncker und Humblot, Leipzig 1908. English translation by Kurt H. Wolff, *The Sociology of Georg Simmel*, Free Press of Glencoe, New York/Collier-Macmillan, London 1964, p. 343.

23   *Ibid.*, p. 339.

24   *Ibid.*

25   *Ibid.*, pp. 340–1.

26   *Ibid.*, p. 342.

List of Illustrations

64 Chanel in front of a portfolio of wedding dresses, 1937.
Photo Roger Schall. Collection of the artist.

65 Coco Chanel and Muriel Maxwell, photographed by Horst, 1938.
Collection Chanel.
© *Horst.*

66 Patchwork of fashion drawings, 1925/45.
Left to right, top to bottom:
(a) *Original image UFAC. Photo Dominique Genet. Drawing by Vertès appeared in* Harper's Bazaar, *April 1939.*
© *A.D.A.G.P.*
(b) *Original image UFAC. Photo Dominique Genet. Drawing by Christian Bérard.* Vogue, *October 1937.*
© *Condé Nast Publications.*
© *SPADEM.*
(c) *Original image UFAC. Photo Dominique Genet. Drawing by Gabrielle Chanel. 1935/40.*
(d) *Original image UFAC. Photo Dominique Genet. Drawing by Gabrielle Chanel. 1935/40.*
(e) *Original image UFAC. Photo Dominique Genet. Drawing by Gabrielle Chanel. 1935/40.*
(f) *Original image UFAC. Photo Dominique Genet. Drawing appeared in* Art, Goût et Beauté, *September 1930.*
(g) *Original image UFAC. Photo Dominique Genet. Drawing appeared in* Vogue, *September 1929.* © *Condé Nast Publications.*
(h) *Original image UFAC. Photo Dominique Genet. Drawing by Vertès appeared in* Harper's Bazaar, *April 1939.*
© *A.D.A.G.P.*
(i) *Original image UFAC. Photo Dominique Genet. Drawing by Gabrielle Chanel. 1930/35.*

67 Chanel's hands, photographed by François Kollar, 1937.
Ministère de la Culture, Paris.

A SHOWER OF STARS

68 Diamond necklace and diadem on a wax mannequin, Chanel 1932.
Photo Harlingue-Viollet.

69 Study for a necklace by Paul Iribe, *c.* 1925/30.
Original image and photo Bibliothèque Forney.

70 Diamond brooches and diadem on a wax mannequin, Chanel, 1932.
Photo Harlingue-Viollet.

71 Chanel brooch, *c.* 1955.
Photo Patrick Jacob.

72 Diamond bracelet, Chanel, 1932.
Plate from the catalogue Bijoux de diamants, *Chanel, Imprimerie Draeger, November 1932. Original image Chanel. Photo Robert Bresson.*

Diamond necklace, Chanel, 1932.
Plate from the catalogue Bijoux de diamants, *Chanel, Imprimerie Draeger, November 1932. Original image Chanel. Photo Robert Bresson.*

73 Illustration by Paul Iribe for the magazine *Choix,* June 1930.
Original image and photo Bibliothèque Forney.

Study for a necklace by Paul Iribe, *c.* 1925/30.
Original image and photo Bibliothèque Forney.

74 Diamond diadem, Chanel, 1932.
Plate from the catalogue Bijoux de diamants, *Chanel, Imprimerie Draeger, November 1932. Original image Chanel. Photo Robert Bresson.*

75 The sparkling scene at the 1932 exhibition in the Rue du Faubourg-Saint-Honoré.
Photo André Kertész. © *Ministère de la Culture - France (AFDPP). Reproduced in* Vogue Paris, *January 1933.*

76 Diamond necklace, Chanel, 1932.
Plate from the catalogue Bijoux de diamants, *Chanel, Imprimerie Draeger, November 1932. Original image Chanel. Photo Robert Bresson.*

77 Headband, signed Chanel, *c.* 1960.
Original image Chanel. Photo Dominique Genet.

Headband, signed Chanel, *c.* 1960.
Original image Chanel. Photo Dominique Genet.

LANDSCAPES OF FANTASY

78 Gold, amethyst and emerald ring, and cigarette box with a lid of rubies and white and blue sapphires.
All rights reserved.

79 Chanel.
Photo Roger Schall. Collection of the artist.

80 Necklace.
Original image and photo Chanel.

81 Bracelet.
Original image and photo Chanel.

82 *Leaf* brooch, 1935/38.
Collection Billy Boy.

Scroll earrings.
Original image and photo Chanel.

Stylized Flower brooch, 1928/35.
Collection Billy Boy.

83 Drawing by Giorgio de Chirico for a *Vogue* cover, December 1935, showing jewelry by Chanel. A rope of pearls is intertwined with a short garnet necklace mounted on a twist of gold.
Original image Chanel. Photo Dominique Genet. © *Condé Nast Publications.* © *SPADEM.*

84 Illustration from *Vogue,* April 1938. *Bijoux de Fleurs* (Flower Jewelry): four pieces by Chanel, one by Schiaparelli, one by Paquin.
Original image UFAC. Photo Dominique Genet. © *Condé Nast Publications.*

85 Chanel necklace on a wax mannequin, 1938.
Photo Roger Schall. Collection of the artist.

Flower necklace.
All rights reserved.

86   *Palm Tree* brooch.
     Original image and photo
     Chanel.

     Trafalgar-Picadilly [*sic*]
     brooch.
     Original image and photo
     Chanel.

87   Chanel crossing the Rue
     Cambon.
     Photo Hatami. Original image
     Chanel.

     FRIENDSHIP WITH VERDURA

88   Coco Chanel and Fulco di
     Verdura in 1937.
     Photo Lipnitzki-Viollet.

89   Bracelet, *c.* 1960.
     Original image Chanel. Photo
     Dominique Genet.

     Bracelet, *c.* 1960.
     Original image Chanel. Photo
     Dominique Genet.

90   Two bracelets executed by
     Fulco di Verdura, *c.* 1937.
     Photo courtesy Verdura, New
     York.

     Brooch executed by Fulco di
     Verdura, 1925/32.
     Photo Christie's, New York.

91   Coco Chanel, *c.* 1937.
     Photo François Kollar.
     Ministère de la Culture, Paris.

92   *Effigy* brooch executed by Fulco
     di Verdura, signed Chanel,
     1925/38.
     Collection Billy Boy.

     Sea-horse brooch executed by
     Fulco di Verdura, signed Chanel,
     1933/38.
     Collection Billy Boy.

93   *Rose* brooch executed by Fulco
     di Verdura, signed Chanel, 1935.
     Original image and photo
     Chanel.

     AFTER THE WAR

94   Pendant cross on Chanel chain,
     1954/71.
     Workshop of Robert Goossens,
     Paris. Collection Robert
     Goossens. Photo Kim.

95   Twisted gold bracelet and cuff
     bracelet, Chanel, 1954/71.
     Workshop of Robert Goossens,
     Paris. Collection Robert
     Goossens. Photo Kim.

96   Earrings, bracelet and barrette,
     Chanel, 1954/71.
     Workshop of Robert Goossens,
     Paris. Collection Robert
     Goossens. Photo Kim.

97   Open-work brooch, signed
     Chanel, 1954/71.
     Collection Billy Boy.

98   Turquoise sautoir and brooch,
     Chanel, 1954/71.
     Collection Robert Goossens.
     Photo Kim.

99   Gold, baroque pearl, turquoise
     and tourmaline cross (obverse
     and reverse), 1960s.
     Workshop of Robert Goossens,
     Paris. Collection Robert Goossens.
     Photo Dominique Genet.

100 Brooch and necklace, Chanel,
     1954/71.
     Workshop of Robert Goossens,
     Paris. Collection Robert
     Goossens. Photo Kim.

101 Gold cross engraved with a saint
     in Byzantine style, 1954/71.
     Workshop of Robert Goossens,
     Paris. Collection Robert Goossens.
     Photo Dominique Genet.

102 Cross of gold and four rock
     crystals, 1954/71.
     Workshop of Robert Goossens,
     Paris. Collection Robert Goossens.
     Photo Dominique Genet.

103 Cross of gold and five rock
     crystals, 1954/71.
     Workshop of Robert Goossens,
     Paris. Collection Robert Goossens.
     Photo Dominique Genet.

     THE SPIRIT OF THE AGES

104 Bracelet from Yakmur (Syria),
     third century.
     Musée du Louvre, Paris,
     Collection de Clerq. Photo
     Réunion des Musées
     Nationaux.

105 Bracelet executed by Robert
     Goossens for Mlle Chanel,
     1954/71.
     Collection Robert Goossens.
     Photo Kim.

     Merovingian fibula from
     Humbécourt (Haute-Marne),
     eighth century.
     Musée de Saint-Germain-en-
     Laye. Photo Réunion des
     Musées Nationaux.

106 Chanel necklace, 1954/71.
     Collection Robert Goossens.
     Photo Kim.

107 Chanel necklaces.
     Collection Billy Boy.

108 Cross of the Knights of Malta,
     sixteenth century.
     Musée de la Légion d'Honneur,
     Paris.

     Brooch in the form of a Maltese
     cross, 1928/35.
     Collection Billy Boy. Formerly
     Collection Gripoix.

     Chanel cuff bracelet with
     Maltese cross, *c.* 1950.
     Collection Billy Boy.

109 Coco Chanel at work.
     Photo Hatami. Original image
     Chanel.

110 Hans Holbein the Younger,
     Anne of Cleves (detail), 1539.
     Musée du Louvre, Paris. Photo
     Giraudon.

     Byzantine clasp in the form of a
     Greek cross, sixth century.
     Museo Nazionale del Bargello,
     Florence. Photo Giraudon.

111 Brooch and earrings, Chanel,
     1954/71.
     Collection Robert Goossens.
     Photo Kim.

112 Veronese, *Portrait of a Woman*
     (detail), 1528/88.
     Musée de la Chartreuse,
     Douai. Photo Giraudon.

     Chanel brooch, *c.* 1960.
     Original image Chanel. Photo
     Dominique Genet.

113 Articulated necklace executed
     by Gripoix for Chanel.
     Collection Billy Boy.

114 Two bracelets.
     © *Christie's Images (Sale*
     1978: Chanel's personal
     collection).

     Rigid collar, signed Chanel,
     c. 1960.
     Workshop of Robert Goossens,
     Paris. Original image Chanel.
     Photo Dominique Genet.

115 Belt of gilded fabric, Chanel,
     1954/71.
     Collection Robert Goossens.
     Photo Kim.

ACKNOWLEDGMENTS

The publishers would like to express their gratitude to the following for the helpful advice and information that they have provided in the preparation of this work:

Roger Boujeat (Desrues), Billy Boy, Mylène Bresson, Odile Charbonneau (*Marie Claire*), Véronique Damagnez (Condé Nast Archives), Isabelle du Pasquier (Musée de la Légion d'Honneur), Marie-Odile Dutsch (Sotheby's, Paris), Robert Goossens, Josette Gripoix, Pamela Harris, Betty Jais, Lilou Marquand, Daniela Mascetti (Sotheby's, London), Sylvie Pitoiset (Bibliothèque Forney), Roger Schall, Jessica Thomas (Christie's, London), Amanda Triossi, Françoise Vittu (Musée de la Mode de la Ville de Paris), Jack Palmer White, Rainer Wick.

Bibliography

BOOKS

Raymond Bachollet, Daniel Bordet, Anne-Claude Lelieur, *Paul Iribe*, Denoël, Paris, 1982.

Edmonde Charles-Roux, *Chanel*, Knopf, New York, 1975/Collins Harvill, London, 1989.

Edmonde Charles-Roux, *Chanel and Her World*, Weidenfeld and Nicolson, London, 1981.

Jean Cocteau, *A Portfolio of Fashion and Theatre Designs*, The Chelsea Press, London, 1989.

Claude Delay, *Chanel solitaire*, Gallimard, Paris, 1983.

Pierre Galante, *Les Années Chanel*, Mercure de France, Paris, 1972.

Marcel Haedrich, *Coco Chanel*, Belfond, Paris, 1987.

A. Kenneth Snowman (ed.), *The Master Jewelers*, Thames and Hudson, London, 1990.

Jean Leymarie, *Chanel*, Skira, Geneva, 1987.

Lilou Marquand, *Chanel m'a dit*, J.C. Lattès, Paris, 1990.

Paul Morand, *L'Allure de Chanel*, Hermann, Paris, 1976.

Paul Morand, *Venises*, Gallimard, Paris, 1971.

Sylvie Raulet, *Jewelry of the 1940s and 1950s*, Thames and Hudson, London, 1988.

Misia Sert, *Two or Three Muses: The Memoirs of Misia Sert*, Museum Press, London, 1953.

Georg Simmel, *The Sociology of Georg Simmel*, Free Press of Glencoe, New York/Collier-Macmillan, London, 1964.

SALE AND EXHIBITION CATALOGUES

Paul Iribe, précurseur de l'art décoratif, 1883/1935, exhibition from 6 October to 31 December 1983, Bibliothèque Forney.

Mademoiselle Chanel, exhibition from 20 November to 22 December 1990, Bunkamura Museum of Fine Arts, Tokyo.

Collection Boris Kochno, sale of 11 and 12 October 1991, Sotheby's, Monaco.

NEWSPAPER AND MAGAZINE ARTICLES

Vogue, September 1925, January 1933, June 1935, June 1938, March 1954, November 1954, March 1971, August 1971.

L'Intransigeant, 26 October 1932, 8 November 1932.

Candide, 10 November 1932.

Les Annales, 18 November 1932.

Marie Claire, March 1956.

L'Express, August 1956.

Paris-Match, December 1958.

The Sunday Times Magazine, 1 October 1967.

The Connoisseur, June 1987.

Index

Numerals in *italics* refer to captions